AIR
&
OTHER
GASES

Robert C. Mebane
Thomas R. Rybolt

Illustrations by Anni Matsick

TWENTY-FIRST CENTURY BOOKS

A Division of Henry Holt and Company
New York

Twenty-First Century Books
A Division of Henry Holt and Company, Inc.
115 West 18th Street
New York, NY 10011

Henry Holt® and colophon are trademarks of
Henry Holt and Company, Inc.
Publishers since 1866

Library of Congress Cataloging-in-Publication Data

Mebane, Robert C.
Air and other gases / Robert C. Mebane and Thomas R. Rybolt;
illustrations by Anni Matsick.—1st ed.
p. cm. — (Everyday material science experiments)
Includes bibliographical references and index.
1. Gases—Juvenile literature. 2. Gases—Experiments—Juvenile literature.
3. Air—Juvenile literature. 4. Air—Experiments—Juvenile literature.
[1. Gases—Experiments. 2. Air—Experiments. 3. Experiments.]
I. Rybolt, Thomas R. II. Matsick, Anni, ill. III. Title. IV. Series:
Mebane, Robert C. Everyday Material Science Experiments.
QC161.2.M43   1995
530.4'3'078—dc20   94–24959
                                                              CIP
                                                               AC

ISBN 0–8050–2839–0
First Edition 1995

Designed by Kelly Soong

Printed in Mexico
All first editions are printed on acid-free paper ∞.
10 9 8 7 6 5 4 3 2 1

For Marty and Linda, with love   —R.M.

*For my aunt, Eloise Rybolt, and the memory of
my uncle, Don Rybolt*   —T.R.

ACKNOWLEDGMENT

We wish to thank Professor Mickey Sarquis of Miami University, Middletown, Ohio, for reading and making helpful comments on the manuscript.

CONTENTS

INTRODUCTION

The world around you is filled with *Air and Other Gases, Water and Other Liquids, Salts and Solids, Metals,* and *Plastics and Polymers.* Some of these materials are part of our natural environment, and some are part of our created, industrial environment. The materials that we depend on for life and the materials that are part of our daily living all have distinct properties. These properties can be best understood through careful examination and experimentation.

Have you ever wondered how a fluorescent lightbulb works, how a fire burns and can be extinguished, why lightning flashes through the air, or why you can hear the sea in some seashells? In this book you will discover the answers to these and many other fascinating questions about *Air and Other Gases.* In the process you will learn about gases as materials—what they are made of, how they behave, and why they are important.

Each experiment is designed to stand alone. That is, it's not necessary to start with the first experiment and proceed to the second, then the third, and so on. Feel free to skip around—that's part of the fun of discovery. As you do the experiments, think about the results and what they mean to you. Also, think about how the results apply to the world around you.

At the beginning of each experiment, you will find one or more icons identifying the important physical science concepts dealt with in the experiment. For example, if the icon ❋ appears at the top of the page, it means that matter, one of the basic concepts of science, will be explored. On page 60, you will find a listing of all the icons—matter, energy, light, heat, sound, and electricity—and the experiments to which they relate.

As you carry out the experiments in this book, be sure to follow carefully any special safety instructions that are given. **For some experiments, a ❶ means that you should have an adult work with you**. For all your experiments, you need to make sure that an adult knows what you are doing. Remember to clean up after your experiment is completed.

AIR PRESSURE

MATERIALS NEEDED

Small drinking glass

Water

Spoon

Index card(s)

What is all around you, but you cannot see it? *Air*. The air that is around you has weight and pushes on you in all directions. To learn more, try this experiment.

Fill a small drinking glass nearly all the way with water and place it on the countertop next to a sink. Using a spoon, continue to add water to the glass until the level of the water bulges just above the rim of the glass. Starting at one edge of the glass, begin sliding a dry index card over the rim of the glass, as shown in Figure A. You want to avoid trapping any large air bubbles under the card as you slide it over the rim of the glass. Continue sliding the card until it completely covers the rim of the glass and overhangs the other side by about 1 in. (between 2 and 3 cm). Some water will spill down the sides of the glass as you slide the card across the rim of the glass.

Without touching the card, hold the glass up and look through the glass to see if any large air bubbles are trapped under the card. If there are large bubbles present, repeat the whole process using a dry index card. Air bubbles in the glass may change the results of the experiment.

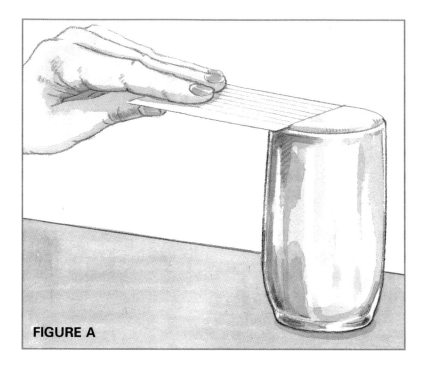

FIGURE A

Hold your covered glass of water over the sink. Turn the glass upside down. What happens to the glass of water?

When you turn the covered glass of water upside down, you should find that the water does not spill out of the glass but remains in the glass (if the water spills out, repeat the experiment with a dry index card and make sure no large air bubbles are trapped under the card). You might think that gravity should pull on the index card and the water in the glass and cause the water to pour from the glass. This does not happen because air pressure pushes on the index card. This air pressure holds the card against the upside-down glass of water.

Air pressure is a force pushing on the surface of the earth. It is caused by the earth's gravity pulling on the air in the atmosphere. Also known as *atmospheric pressure*, air pressure varies with weather and altitude but is approximately 14.7 lb per sq in. (1.03 kg per sq cm) at sea level. Air pressure is also commonly expressed in inches of mercury, millimeters of mercury, and atmospheres. A device called a *barometer* is used to measure air pressure.

To better understand the size or magnitude of air pressure, let's compare it to the pressure exerted by a quarter. On a perfectly flat table, a quarter exerts a pressure of only 0.0018 lb per sq in. (0.00013 kg per sq cm). It would take a stack of more than 800 quarters to equal the pressure exerted by the air. A stack of 800 quarters would stand over 4.7 ft (1.4 m) high.

In this experiment the water in the inverted glass does not spill because the weight of the water in the glass is much less than the weight of the air pressing on the index card covering the glass. The weight of air pressing on the index card covering an average small drinking glass is about 74 lb (34 kg). The weight of water in an average small drinking glass holding 1 cup (0.24 l) of water is only about 0.5 lb (0.2 kg). Thus, the pressure exerted on the index card by the air is nearly 150 times greater than the pressure exerted by the water in the glass. The index card is pressed so firmly against the inverted glass that no air can enter the glass, so no water can spill out.

Do you think the size or shape of the container of water will make a difference in this experiment?

PUSH OF AIR

MATERIALS NEEDED

Water

Measuring cup

Empty plastic milk jug (gallon size)

Microwave oven

Oven mitt

❗ **Alert! Adult supervision needed.**

In this experiment you will try to observe the effect of the pressure caused by the air around us.

Fill a sink with cool tap water.

Add 1 cup (0.24 l) of water to an empty gallon-size milk jug. **This must be a plastic milk jug**. Place the jug sideways in a microwave oven, as shown in Figure A. **Never put metal objects into a microwave oven, because they could damage the microwave oven while operating. Do not put the top on the plastic jug. It must be left open when heated.** Close the oven and set the microwave to heat the water on a setting of high for 3 minutes.

At the end of 3 minutes, open the microwave oven and screw or snap the top on the plastic jug. **Be careful. The water and the jug are hot**. Use an oven mitt to remove the jug and immediately place it in the sink of cool water. Watch the jug. What happens?

You should see the plastic jug collapse when it is placed in the sink of water. Can you explain why this happens?

The water inside the jug is heated in the microwave until it boils. As the water in the jug boils, the liquid changes to vapor, or steam. The steam expands to fill the jug and pushes air out. The air inside the jug is replaced with steam. When you place the cap on the jug and close it, the steam is trapped inside.

When the jug is placed in the sink of cool water, the steam in the jug is cooled and changes from a gas back to a liquid. Liquid water takes up much less room than the hot water vapor. As a result, the pressure inside the jug decreases and becomes less than the room air pressure. The pressure of the room air pushes on the surface of the jug and causes it to collapse. The sides of the jug are pushed in just as if you had squeezed the jug with your hands.

The earth is surrounded by a sea of air. We live at the bottom of this sea of air, which we call the atmosphere. This air is held around the earth by the gravitation of the earth. The air in the atmosphere pushes down with a pressure of 14.7 lb per sq in. (1.03 kg per sq cm) at sea level and less as you go to higher altitudes. We do not normally notice this push of air because it is all around us and inside us.

Just as the air has pressure, so does the water in oceans and lakes. Submarines must be able to withstand the pressure of water above them. Submersibles are diving vehicles that can withstand even greater pressures than submarines and go to greater depths. In 1960 a type of submersible vehicle called a *bathyscaphe* went to a depth of almost 35,800 ft (10,920 m) in the Pacific Ocean.

This bathyscaphe had a steel sphere attached to a large cylinder filled with gasoline. This cylinder was used to provide flotation so the craft could rise to the surface. Gasoline is less dense than water. In a submarine, air is used for flotation. However, at the great depths of the ocean floor, a cylinder filled with air would be crushed—just like your jug was crushed! This is why submersibles like bathyscaphes can go deeper than submarines. They do not use chambers of air for flotation.

Underwater divers can also be affected by gas pressure. They can be injured if the pressure inside their bodies does not equal the pressure outside. As divers rise to the surface, they must allow time for their bodies to adjust to the lower pressure. Otherwise, the air in their lungs will expand. If this expanding air is forced into their blood, it can form bubbles and block the blood flow. This condition is called an *air embolism* and it can injure or kill a diver.

A related condition is called the *bends*, which occurs when nitrogen gas forms bubbles in the blood of a diver rising too rapidly to the surface. Nitrogen gas from the pressurized air in divers' tanks is dissolved in the blood under high pressure. However, this nitrogen gas can bubble into the blood as the diver rises to the surface. To avoid the bends, divers must rise slowly enough to the surface to allow the nitrogen gas to come slowly out of the blood.

Can you think of other effects of changing gas pressure?

3

POP A TOP

MATTER

MATERIALS NEEDED

Safety goggles (available in hardware stores)

Teaspoon

Vinegar

Plastic film container with snap-on lid (small cylinder used to hold 35-mm film)

Alka-Seltzer tablet

Clock or watch

❗ Alert! Adult supervision needed.

In this experiment you will produce a gas and observe the effect of pressure due to this gas. **You should do this activity either outside or in a kitchen sink. You should wear eye protection (safety goggles) when you do this activity.**

Add 1 teaspoon (5 ml) of vinegar to an empty plastic film container, as shown in Figure A. This type of container is a cylinder 1.2 in. (3 cm) across and 2 in. (5 cm) high. Packages of 35-mm film are sold in this type of container. The lid should snap on and off.

Break an Alka-Seltzer tablet into eight approximately equal pieces. Add one piece (⅛ of the original) of the Alka-Seltzer tablet to the plastic container and immediately snap on the lid. Shake the container one time. Immediately after shaking, set the container in a sink if you are inside or on the ground if you are outside. **Step back.** Watch the container, but **do not look directly over the container**. If nothing happens after 3 minutes, remove the top, empty

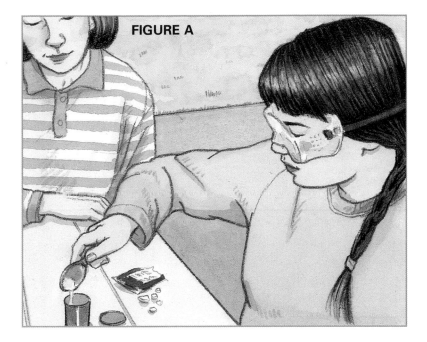

FIGURE A

the container contents, and try again. The top may not have been on completely tight the first time. Repeat the procedure.

What do you observe?

The Alka-Seltzer tablet contains a solid called sodium bicarbonate as well as aspirin and citric acid. When sodium bicarbonate is mixed with water containing an acid such as vinegar, it rapidly produces carbon dioxide gas. Because the Alka-Seltzer tablet contains an acid, it will form carbon dioxide gas when placed in plain water. However, the vinegar helps the gas form more quickly.

The carbon dioxide gas produced inside the plastic container causes the pressure inside the container to increase. When the pressure is great enough, it pushes the top off. You see the top pop off the plastic holder. There may be enough force to cause the top to fly into the air.

If you repeat this experiment, you should find that a smaller piece of Alka-Seltzer produces less gas. A small enough piece will not produce enough gas to pop off the top.

Having the sodium bicarbonate in a tablet (Alka-Seltzer) instead of a powder such as baking soda keeps the carbon dioxide from forming too fast. A powder will react much quicker because most of it comes in contact with the acid immediately. Do you think four small pieces of tablet would react quicker than one bigger piece?

Pressure is a measure of a force, or push, per area. At sea level the pressure of our atmosphere is 14.7 lb per sq in. This pressure is caused by the weight of air in the atmosphere above us. The pressure of the atmosphere decreases as you go to a higher altitude. This decrease in pressure occurs because there is less air above you. Measuring air pressure is used to determine the altitude, or height, of an airplane.

Measuring air pressure is important for owners of automobiles and bicycles. The pressure of the air inside their tires is measured with a tire gauge. This pressure should be several times the pressure of the atmosphere. If the pressure is too low, the tire will not work properly. If the pressure is too high, the tire may burst or blow apart.

Air pressure is also important in a type of brake called an *air brake*, used on buses, trains, and large trucks. Air brakes use high-pressure gas to push on a piston and force a special pad called a *brake shoe* against a wheel. As the brake shoe pushes against the wheel, it causes the wheel to stop turning.

A *compressor* is a type of pump used to force air molecules closer together and increase pressure. Compressed air is stored in a chamber and is used to operate air brakes. For example, each car on a train may have its own tank of compressed air that is used to operate its brakes.

Can you think of other uses for gas at high pressure?

4

DISSOLVED AIR

MATERIALS NEEDED

Two-cup measuring cup

Water

Two saucepans, one with lid

Cooking thermometer

Stove

Paper

Pencil

Large jar with lid

⚠ **Alert! Adult supervision needed.**

Many solids and liquids dissolve in water. Do you think gases can dissolve in water? To find out, try this experiment.

Pour 2 cups (0.48 l) of cold tap water into a saucepan. Place a cooking thermometer in the water and heat the saucepan on the stove using a medium-high setting.

Watch the bottom and the sides of the saucepan inside the pan as the water heats. Do you see any bubbles? Write down the temperature of the cooking thermometer when you first see tiny bubbles form. Continue heating the water until it boils and let it boil for 2 minutes. What is the temperature of the boiling water? Turn off the stove, cover the saucepan with a lid, and allow the water to cool overnight.

The next day, pour the water from the saucepan into a 2-cup measuring cup. How much water was lost by evaporation? Transfer half of the water back into the saucepan and the other half into a jar. Secure the lid on the jar and shake for 45 seconds. Pour the water from the jar into the second saucepan.

Place the cooking thermometer in the saucepan containing the water that was shaken in the jar. Heat the water in both saucepans to boiling using a medium-high setting. Watch for changes in both saucepans. Do tiny bubbles form in both saucepans before the water in each begins to boil? At what temperature do you first see tiny bubbles form inside the saucepan containing the water that was shaken? Is this the same temperature you recorded the day before?

You should find that tiny bubbles form on the bottom and sides of the saucepan shortly after you begin heating the 2 cups of water. These bubbles form well before the water begins to boil. In fact, you should find that the temperature of the water is only 100°F to 140°F (38°C to 60°C) when you start to see the tiny bubbles.

Water boils at 212°F (100°C) at sea level and slightly less at higher elevations. When water boils, water in the liquid state changes into water in the gaseous state (steam). The bubbles you see in boiling water are made of steam.

You should notice that as the water starts to boil, fewer and larger bubbles form in the saucepan. When you heat the two portions of water the next morning, you should find that tiny bubbles only form in the water that was shaken in a jar. Why didn't tiny bubbles form in the other sample of water?

When you think of substances dissolving in water, you normally think of solids and liquids. But gases, too, can dissolve in water. Air, which is a mixture of mostly nitrogen and oxygen gases, readily dissolves in water.

Solubility is a term used to describe how much of one substance dissolves in another substance. Many factors, including temperature, affect the solubility of substances in water. The solubility of most solids and liquids is greater in warm water than in cold water. Can you think of examples? The opposite is true for gases—more gas will dissolve in cold water than in warm water.

You can observe this by opening both an ice-cold carbonated soft drink and one that is at room temperature. Which one produces more "swish" when it is opened?

In this experiment the tiny bubbles you saw shortly after you started heating the 2 cups of water were bubbles of air. As the temperature of the water in the pan increased, the solubility of the air in the water decreased and bubbles formed.

When you boiled the water for 2 minutes, you completely removed all the air that was originally dissolved. The next day, when you heated the portion of water that was not shaken in the jar, no tiny air bubbles formed in the water prior to boiling. By shaking the other portion of the water in a jar, you dissolved air back into the water. This is why you saw tiny bubbles appear in this water shortly after heating.

Fish and certain other aquatic life depend on dissolved oxygen in the water in order to survive. For example, trout can exist only in water that is high in dissolved oxygen. This is why trout are found only in cold, tumbling streams. The tumbling waters constantly put air into (aerate) the cold water, which favors oxygen solubility.

Fish kills have been known to occur in shallow ponds and lakes in the hot summer. As the water in a shallow pond or lake heats up under the summer sun, less oxygen dissolves in the water. The loss of dissolved oxygen in the water can threaten the lives of fish living in the water. Can you think of a way to keep enough dissolved oxygen in a pond in the summertime?

Another way to tell that air is dissolved in water is to freeze the water. Remove an ice cube from the freezer. If you look carefully, you will see tiny air bubbles collected near the center of the ice cube. Why do you think the air bubbles collect in the center of the ice cube?

COOLING GAS

HEAT   MATTER

MATERIALS NEEDED

Paper

Pencil

Outdoor thermometer

Hair spray in spray
can

❶ Alert! Adult supervision needed. Read carefully the warning label on a can of hair spray. The material in the can is flammable and should never be used around a flame or heat source. Do not spray in eyes or mouth.

Air conditioning can make a car or room feel cool and comfortable on a hot, humid day. In this experiment you will explore the principle behind air conditioning with simply a can of hair spray.

Do this experiment outdoors when there is little wind. Record the temperature of the thermometer. Shake the can of hair spray for a few seconds. While holding the nozzle of the spray can about 2 in. (5 cm) from the bulb of the thermometer, as shown in Figure A, spray the bulb with the hair spray for 2 seconds. After a brief pause (1 second), spray the bulb again for 2 seconds. Repeat a third time. Record the temperature of the thermometer immediately after the third spraying. Has the thermometer temperature changed?

Spray cans, like the one you used in this experiment, consist of the product to be dispensed and a propellant. The product,

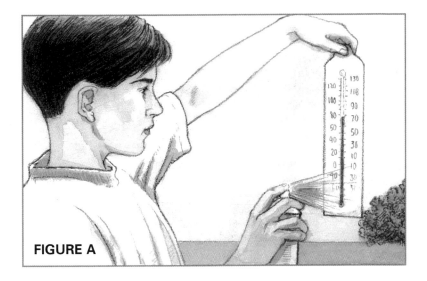

FIGURE A

which is usually a liquid, is forced out of the can and through a nozzle at a high speed by the propellant. As the liquid product passes through the nozzle, it changes into a fine mist called an *aerosol*.

Spray cans are pressurized, meaning the gas pressure inside the can is greater than the air pressure outside the can. Proper operation of the spray can depends on this difference in pressure. Gases always flow from an area of high pressure to an area of low pressure. Thus, as long as the pressure inside the spray can is greater than the pressure outside it, the gas inside the can will spew from the nozzle along with the product in the can.

The gas pressure in a spray can is maintained by the propellant. In most spray cans a volatile (low boiling, easily evaporated) liquid is used as the propellant. Most of the propellant in the can exists as a liquid. However, at normal temperatures some propellant evaporates and exits as a gas above the liquid. The gaseous propellant provides the high pressure in the can.

When the nozzle is pressed, the gas pressure inside the can forces the product and some of the liquid propellant up a tube and out the nozzle. To keep the pressure high while the nozzle is open, the liquid propellant in the can boils, producing more gaseous propellant. When the nozzle closes, the liquid propellant continues to boil until the normal pressure in the can is reached.

There are two reasons why the spray coming from the can in this experiment is cold. The major reason is that some of the liquid propellant in the can exits with the product. This liquid propellant immediately evaporates upon exiting the nozzle. The evaporation of a liquid causes cooling. This is why you may feel cold before toweling yourself dry after taking a bath or shower. The water on your skin evaporates and causes your skin to cool down. Can you think of other examples of the evaporation of a liquid causing cooling?

The other reason for the cooling effect seen in this experiment is less important. Anytime a gas moves from a region of high pressure to a region of low pressure, a cooling of the gas occurs. In this experiment, the gaseous propellant exiting the nozzle experiences a pressure drop that causes some cooling of the gaseous propellant.

Freons, also known as chlorofluorocarbons, were once used as propellants in spray cans but were phased out in the 1980s. Do you know why they are no longer used? Today, many spray cans use either propane, butane, or isobutane or a mixture of these substances. Read the label of several spray cans and see whether you can determine what propellant is used.

Air conditioners work by the same principle explored in this experiment. Shown in Figure B is a diagram of a typical air-conditioning system. At the heart of the system is a compressor that circulates a refrigerant, typically a Freon, through pipes connected in a loop. The refrigerant enters the compressor as a gas at a low pressure, then it exits as a high-pressure gas and enters a condenser, which is outdoors. A fan blows air over the condenser, which removes heat from the gaseous refrigerant and changes it into a liquid. The liquid refrigerant then travels to an evaporator inside the house where the refrigerant evaporates, making the

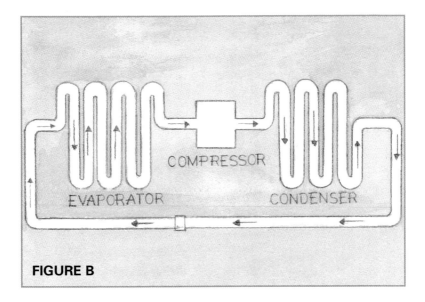

FIGURE B

evaporator cold. Warm air from inside the house is cooled as it is blown over the evaporator. The cooled air is returned to the inside of the house and the gaseous refrigerant exits the evaporator and enters the compressor to begin another cycle.

GASES MOVING THROUGH A BALLOON

MATTER

MATERIALS NEEDED

Measuring cup

Vinegar

Empty 2-liter plastic
  bottle

Small funnel

Tablespoon

Baking soda

Two large balloons

Toothpick or small
  straw

Felt pen

Which gas passes through a balloon faster—air or carbon dioxide? Try this experiment to find out.

Pour 1 cup (0.24 l) of vinegar into an empty 2-liter plastic soda bottle. Using a small funnel, add 2 tablespoons (30 ml) of baking soda to a balloon. A toothpick or small straw may be useful in pushing the baking soda into the balloon.

Fit the balloon over the mouth of the bottle, as shown in Figure A, and while holding the balloon firmly on the neck of the bottle, turn the balloon up to allow the baking soda in the balloon to fall into the bottle. The balloon should start to inflate immediately. Some of the foam produced in the bottle may rise into the balloon, but this will not change the experiment.

When the bubbling in the bottle ceases, carefully remove the balloon from the bottle so as to avoid gas escaping from the balloon. Tie the balloon closed tightly and use a felt pen to label the

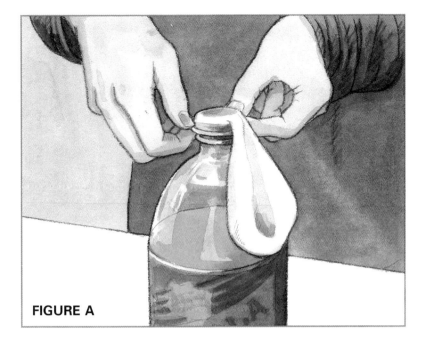

FIGURE A

balloon CO_2. Blow into the second balloon to inflate it with air. When the second balloon is inflated to the size of the balloon labeled CO_2 tie the balloon closed and label it *air*. Place both balloons on a table where they will not be disturbed. Once an hour for 5 hours, observe the size of each balloon. Does one of them shrink faster than the other? How could you use a piece of string to measure how much each balloon shrinks in 5 hours?

The balloon labeled CO_2 is filled mostly with carbon dioxide gas (CO_2 is the chemical formula for *carbon dioxide*). What else do you think might be inside the balloon? The carbon dioxide gas is produced by a chemical reaction that takes place between the baking soda and the vinegar. The balloon attached to the top of the bottle traps the carbon dioxide gas and becomes inflated. The balloon labeled air contains mostly nitrogen (78 percent) and oxygen (21 percent), the major components of air.

You should find that the balloon filled with mostly carbon dioxide shrinks faster than the balloon filled with air. The balloon rubber is permeable to gases. This means that gases can pass through the rubber. Although both air (nitrogen and oxygen) and carbon dioxide can pass through the wall of the balloon, carbon dioxide passes through more quickly. This is why the balloon filled with carbon dioxide shrinks faster.

Many fresh foods in a grocery store are packaged in plastic films, which protect the food by serving as a barrier against things that could cause deterioration, such as dust, microorganisms, light, water, and oxygen in the air. Oxygen can cause certain foods, such as those containing fat and oils, to become rancid quickly, so these foods are usually packaged in a plastic film that prevents oxygen from going through it.

Can you think of other uses of plastic films that are less permeable to oxygen or other gases?

MATTER

FLYING PING-PONG BALL

MATERIALS NEEDED

Hand-held hair dryer

Ping-Pong ball

Have you ever watched a bird or a plane glide through the air with ease and wondered what keeps them aloft? In this experiment you will study the principle of flight without leaving the ground.

Although any hand-held hair dryer may work, you will find this experiment works best with one having a cylindrical nozzle. Turn the hair dryer's fan on high and its temperature on cool. Hold the dryer with its nozzle pointing straight up (vertical). Next, release a Ping-Pong ball 4 to 6 in. (10 to 15 cm) above the nozzle, as shown in Figure A. What happens to the Ping-Pong ball? Does changing the hair dryer's fan speed make a difference in what happens to the ball? What happens if you bring a finger close to the suspended Ping-Pong ball?

Tilt the hair dryer to the left and right, forward and backward. What happens? How far can you tilt the hair dryer before the Ping-Pong ball falls to the floor? Can you estimate this tilt angle?

When you place the Ping-Pong ball in the stream of air exiting the hair dryer, you should find that the Ping-Pong ball remains suspended above the dryer. As you tilt the dryer, the Ping-Pong ball remains suspended, even though the hair dryer is

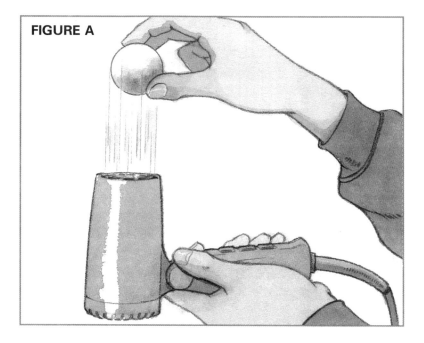

FIGURE A

no longer directly under the ball. You may find that sometimes the Ping-Pong ball spins rapidly in the stream of air.

Daniel Bernoulli, a Swiss mathematician, made an important discovery in the eighteenth century that helps explain your observations in this experiment. Working with fluids, Bernoulli found that the pressure exerted by a fluid becomes less as the fluid moves faster. This is known as Bernoulli's principle. Moving air, which behaves as a fluid, obeys Bernoulli's principle—the faster the air moves, the less pressure it exerts.

When you release the Ping-Pong ball above the hair dryer, the air stream exiting the hair dryer pushes on the Ping-Pong ball, holding it directly above the dryer. The Ping-Pong ball does not fall to one side of the dryer because of Bernoulli's principle.

As shown in Figure B, a portion of the air stream strikes and moves over the surface of the Ping-Pong ball (curved lines) while some of the air stream rushes past the ball (straight lines). The air moving over the surface of the Ping-Pong ball and the air rushing

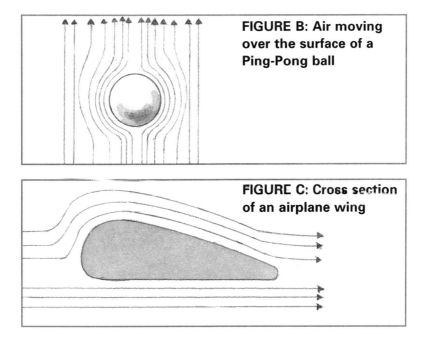

FIGURE B: Air moving over the surface of a Ping-Pong ball

FIGURE C: Cross section of an airplane wing

by the ball arrive at the top of the ball at the same time. Since the Ping-Pong ball is curved, the air moving over the surface travels a greater distance, and at a faster speed, than the air rushing by the ball. According to Bernoulli's principle, since the air moving over the surface of the Ping-Pong ball is moving faster, it has a lower pressure than the air rushing by the ball. The higher pressure surrounds all sides of the ball and pushes on it, keeping it directly above the hair dryer.

When you tilt the hair dryer, the air exiting the dryer no longer pushes directly underneath the Ping-Pong ball to support it. Instead, the ball is suspended due to Bernoulli's principle. The air moving over the upper surface of the Ping-Pong ball travels faster and has a lower pressure than the air moving over the lower surface of the ball, which exerts a greater pressure. The greater pressure beneath the ball gives the ball "lift" and keeps the ball suspended in air.

An airplane uses Bernoulli's principle to achieve the lift

needed for flight. Figure C shows the cross section of an airplane wing, which is called an *airfoil*. Notice that the upper surface of the wing is curved. As a result of this curvature, the air flowing over the wing travels faster along the upper surface than the flat lower surface, causing the air pressure below the wing to be greater than the air pressure above the wing. This difference forces the wing upward. The upward force on the wing is known as *lift*.

Can you think of other examples of Bernoulli's principle?

FLOATING BAG

MATTER **HEAT**

MATERIALS NEEDED

Large black plastic
  trash bag

Thin string

Scissors

Board

The hot-air balloon was invented in France in 1783 by two brothers, Joseph Michel and Jacques Étienne Montgolfier. On its first voyage carrying people, the Montgolfiers' hot-air balloon flew nearly 5 mi (8 km). Hot-air balloons are still flown today, but mostly for sport. In this experiment you will explore the principle behind hot-air balloon flight.

This experiment works best on a cool, bright, sunny, windless day. Also, try to use the thinnest trash bag you can find.

Open a large black plastic trash bag, and pull it through the air to fill it, as shown in Figure A. Once it is full, gather the edges of the open end together to close the bag. Ask a friend to help you tie the bag closed. Attach one end of thin string about 3 ft (approximately 1 m) long to the closed end of the bag. Use scissors to trim any extra plastic and string from around where the bag is tied closed. Do not cut off the long end of the string.

Locate a sunny spot outside where you can place the plastic bag. Tie the loose end of the string attached to the bag to a board and place the board and plastic bag on the ground. Watch the bag

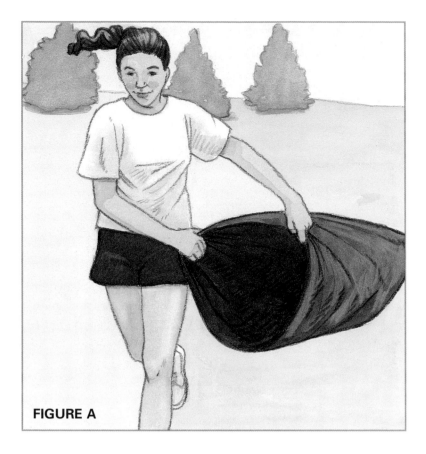

FIGURE A

for a few minutes. What changes take place with the bag? Leave the bag in the sun for several hours, occasionally observing it.

You should find that soon after the bag is placed in the sun, it starts to fill out and tighten up. Also, you should soon start to see it rise off the ground and actually float in the air, held down by the string attached to the board. What do you think is causing the balloon to float?

When you place the black-colored bag in the sun, the surface of the bag heats up. Dark colors absorb light energy and convert it into heat energy. Gradually, the air inside the plastic bag heats up and expands, causing the bag to fill out and tighten up.

Some of the expanded air may even escape the bag where the bag was tied or through the seams.

As air in the bag heats and expands, its density decreases and becomes less than that of the surrounding cooler air. Having a greater density, the surrounding air pushes on the air inside the bag. If the density of the air inside the bag becomes low enough, then the density of the entire bag (air and plastic bag) becomes less than that of the surrounding air and the bag floats. This lifting force is known as *buoyancy* and is similar to the force experienced by a cork floating in water.

What do you think will happen to the floating plastic bag when the sun goes down or no longer shines on the bag? What happens to the density of the air when the bag cools?

The Montgolfier brothers used a straw fire on the ground to heat the air in their first hot-air balloon in 1783. Because the balloon did not carry a heat source during flight, it soon descended back to the ground as the gases in the balloon cooled. Modern hot-air balloons carry a burner and fuel source, usually propane, to maintain the hot gases in the balloons. In addition, modern hot-air balloons are quite large so that they can hold enough hot air to lift not only the fabric of the balloon, but a basket holding passengers, burner, and fuel source. Although the hot-air balloon was invented in 1783, the first hot-air balloon crossing of the Atlantic was achieved only recently, in 1987.

9

FEELING
SOUND WAVES

MATERIALS NEEDED
Stereo and speakers

Have you ever been to a concert or been in a room where loud music was being played and the floor seemed to vibrate to the music? Try this experiment to learn more about why this happens.

Turn on a stereo and either tune in a radio station or play a tape or CD. Hold the back of your hand about 1 in. (2.5 cm) away from the front of one of the speakers. Do you feel anything? Slowly turn the volume up on the stereo and continue holding the back of your hand in front of one of the speakers. You should feel the sound coming from the speaker. If you don't, turn the bass-control knob on the stereo to produce deep bass sounds, and repeat the experiment. Make sure to return the stereo settings to where you found them when you are finished.

Sound is a form of energy that travels in waves. Like the waves produced when a stone is dropped in a pool of water, sound waves consist of alternating ridges and troughs that travel in all directions. The ridges of a sound wave are regions of high air pressure and the troughs are regions of low air pressure.

Sound waves are created anytime an object vibrates. The back-and-forth vibration of an object, such as a string on a guitar, produces the high-pressure and low-pressure regions of a sound wave. To be audible to the average human ear, a sound wave must come from an object vibrating at least 20 times per second and no more than 20,000 times per second. The times an object vibrates per second is known as *frequency*. Deep bass sounds have a low frequency, and high shrill sounds have a high frequency.

In this experiment, you should be able to feel the sound waves coming out the stereo speaker. You may have to turn the volume and bass up on the stereo to produce sound waves strong enough to be felt by your hand. It is easier to feel low-frequency sounds than high-frequency sounds. Why do you think this is the case?

If you have a stereo speaker that has a removable front cover, you can carefully remove the cover and actually see the cone of the speaker vibrate as it produces sound. Do not touch the cone of the speaker, as this may damage it. Make sure to return the speaker cover if you remove it.

Sound cannot travel in a vacuum because there are no molecules in a vacuum to carry the sound wave. Thus, if you were on the moon and you clapped your hands, you would hear no sound. Sound needs a medium to travel through. Air, liquids such as water, and solids are all mediums in which sound can travel. In which of these media do you think sound travels the fastest?

THE SEA
IN A GLASS

SOUND

MATERIALS NEEDED

Glass jar (32-oz. [1-liter] size works well)

Paper towels

Have you ever put a seashell up to your ear and heard what sounded like the roar of the sea? In this activity you will explore the cause of this sound.

Stand in the middle of the kitchen and cover one ear. As shown in Figure A, bring the open end of a glass jar up to your other ear and hold it there as you listen. What do you hear?

Now stuff three or four paper towels into the jar so that they fill the inside of the jar. Once again, stand in the kitchen and cover one ear. Place the open end of the glass jar next to your ear. Listen. What do you hear?

Sound can travel through a solid, liquid, or gas. Most of the time sound travels through the air to reach our ears. People can hear vibrations that cause sound in the range of 20 to 20,000 vibrations per second.

Vibrations cause sound by creating sound waves that travel through the air to our ears. Molecules in the air push nearby molecules, which in turn push others. Sound waves travel through the air because the air expands and contracts at a certain rate, or frequency. A rapid expansion and contraction (high frequency) makes a high-pitched sound. A slower expansion and contraction (slow frequency) makes a deeper sound.

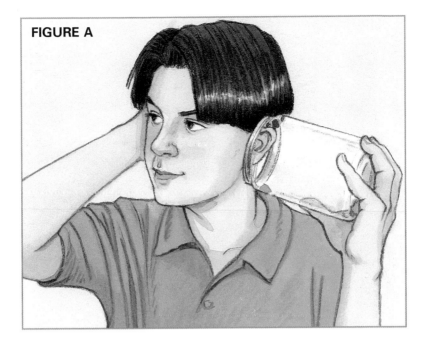

FIGURE A

In this experiment you should hear a deep roaring sound when you place the empty glass jar close to your ear. The sound you hear is made of background noises in the room. The glass jar magnifies the background noise by a process called *resonance*.

Have you ever blown sideways across the top of a bottle and heard a note produced? A note is produced because the air inside the bottle vibrates with a particular frequency. The note or sound is produced because of the resonance of the air in the bottle to that frequency.

If a child is on a swing and someone pushes the swing to make the child go higher, the push must be in resonance. The push is timed to be given just as the swing starts to go forward. The push is at the same frequency as the swing—for example, ten swings a minute and ten pushes a minute. In a similar way, vibrations of sound can be in resonance.

The sounds in the jar are in resonance, or match up, with some of the natural background noise. The background noises in the room air are increased by the resonance of the air in the jar. A kitchen was used for this experiment because there is likely to be some background noise. This experiment does not work well in an extremely quiet room.

In a glass or seashell, some sound waves are in resonance with the background noises in the air. Certain sounds are picked up by the air inside the jar or shell and are magnified. You hear a deep roaring sound. Of course, there is no ocean in the glass or seashell, but the deep roar can easily be imagined to be the sound of a roaring ocean.

What happens when the jar is filled with paper towels? The space inside the jar is filled and the jar becomes quiet. The air in the jar cannot pick up sounds from the air because the paper towels tend to absorb and muffle sounds.

You can demonstrate another interesting example of resonance with a piano. Open a piano so you can see the strings inside. Hold down the sustaining pedal that lifts the hammers off the strings of the piano and sing a note into the open piano. When you stop singing, you will hear the note continue. Some of the piano strings vibrate in resonance, or at the same frequency as the frequency of the note you sang. When you stop singing, these strings continue to vibrate and the sound continues.

Over 100 years ago, Lord Rayleigh (John William Strutt), a British scientist and pioneer in sound research, found that some people, without looking, could judge the size of a room by the resonance of the room. Each room has a certain background sound due to stray noises in it.

You may want to repeat this experiment with other glasses and see how the resonance sound varies with the shape and size of the glass. Can you tell the size of a glass by the resonance sound of the glass? Can you tell the size of the room you are in by the sound of the room?

LIGHT FROM A CHARGED GAS

Have you ever wondered how a fluorescent lightbulb works? Have you ever wondered why lightning flashes through the sky? This experiment may help answer both these questions.

This experiment works best in the winter, when the air is dry. Blow up a balloon and tie it closed. Take the balloon and a fluorescent lightbulb into a room and turn off the lights. **Be careful not to drop or bump the fluorescent lightbulb—it can break.** Rapidly rub the balloon back and forth across your hair or a wool sweater for about 20 seconds. Immediately place the balloon on the fluorescent lightbulb, as shown in Figure A. What do you see?

A fluorescent lightbulb is a glass tube filled with mercury vapor and argon gas at a low pressure. When you rub the balloon on your hair or sweater, it gains extra electrons. Since electrons are negative particles found in atoms, the balloon gains a negative charge. We call this charge on the balloon *static electricity*.

When you touch the fluorescent lightbulb with the charged balloon, the extra electrons flow from the balloon into the bulb. This flow of electrons causes the bulb to give off light. You should see a flash of light come from the fluorescent lightbulb. The light does not last long because there is a limited source of electrons.

When the flow of electrons stops, then the light coming from the gas inside the bulb also stops.

A fluorescent lightbulb has metal at each end called *electrodes*. When a fluorescent bulb in a light fixture is turned on, a steady supply of electrons from an electrical source travels through wires, enters the electrodes, and keeps the bulb lit.

When the bulb is first turned on, the electricity causes the argon gas to ionize, or to change to charged atoms (ions). The current of electricity going through the argon ions helps to remove electrons from the mercury atoms inside the glass bulb. The charged mercury atoms give off ultraviolet and visible light that strikes a special coating on the inside of the glass tube. This coating absorbs the ultraviolet light from the mercury atoms and gives off a white light. It is the white light from this coating inside the tube that you see when the bulb lights up.

In a lightning storm, electrical energy is changed to light. Concentrated static electricity builds until suddenly extra electrons flow through the air. These electrons ionize gas molecules in the air. The ionized molecules give off extra energy as light.

Using a gas to give off light saves energy. A fluorescent bulb only requires about one-fourth as much energy as a regular incandescent bulb. You may notice that incandescent bulbs get extremely hot, but fluorescent bulbs only get warm. The extra energy used by incandescent bulbs is given off as heat rather than light.

FLUORESCENT BULB

INCANDESCENT BULB

FIGURE B

A fluorescent lightbulb is filled with gas at a pressure much lower than the pressure of gas in the air or in a balloon. It is easier for electricity to flow through a gas if the pressure or amount of gas is low. This is why you see a flash of light come from the fluorescent lightbulb but not from the air. The amount of electricity on the balloon is not enough to flow through the air. However, you may see flashes of light in the air if enough static electricity is present.

MAKING
A SPARK

LIGHT   ELECTRICITY

MATERIALS NEEDED

Miniature neon lamp
or simple voltage
tester

Balloon

6-volt lantern battery

Magnifying glass
(optional)

Have you ever wondered how a neon sign works? Have you thought about how a spark plug in an automobile or lawn-mower works? In the following experiment you will study the principle behind a neon sign and the spark plug.

You will need a miniature neon lamp for this experiment. Inexpensive miniature neon lamps can be purchased at Radio Shack or other electronic supply stores. This experiment also works well with a simple voltage tester that contains a neon lamp. Simple voltage testers can be purchased in most hardware stores. (See Figure A.)

To begin the experiment, inflate a balloon and tie it closed. Hold one of the wires, called leads, coming out of the neon lamp in one hand and hold the balloon in the other hand. Rub the balloon rapidly on your hair or on a wool sweater for about 20 seconds. Slowly move the charged balloon to the free end of the neon lamp, as shown in Figure B. What happens to the neon bulb? If you do not see anything, you may want to repeat the experiment in a darkened room. This experiment works best when the air is dry—usually on a cold, sunny winter day.

FIGURE A: Miniature neon lamp and voltage tester

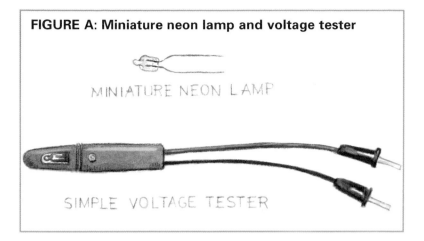

MINIATURE NEON LAMP

SIMPLE VOLTAGE TESTER

FIGURE B

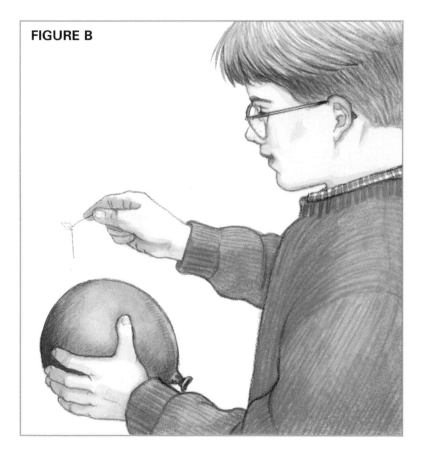

For the second part of the experiment, touch one lead of the neon bulb to the positive terminal and the other lead to the negative terminal of a 6-volt lantern battery. Does the neon bulb glow?

Electricity, which is the flow of electrons, moves easily through metals because metals are good conductors. In contrast, gases, such as air, are poor conductors. Gases are poor conductors because under normal conditions, the atoms or molecules that make up the gas are neutral. This means the atoms and molecules have the same number of negative and positive charges. For a gas to conduct electricity, some of the atoms or molecules of the gas must be made to have a charge, either negative or positive.

A charged atom or molecule is called an *ion*, and the process of changing a neutral atom or molecule into an ion is called *ionization*. Since the atoms or molecules of a gas are normally neutral, it requires energy to ionize a gas.

If you look carefully at the miniature neon lamp you will notice two metal posts, separated by about 0.08 in. (2 mm), enclosed in a glass bulb. Enclosed in the glass bulb are gaseous neon atoms that can be ionized and conduct electricity between the two metal posts. You may find a magnifying glass useful for looking at the miniature neon bulb.

Two different sources of electricity are used in this experiment. The first source is a rubber balloon, which is electrically charged by rubbing it on your hair or a wool sweater. The balloon becomes charged because electrons are removed from your hair or sweater and go onto the inflated balloon as you rub the balloon. This is a form of electricity called static electricity because the electrical charge is stationary. The second source of electricity used in this experiment is a battery. The electricity or flow of electrons is produced in a battery by a series of chemical reactions.

When the charged balloon is brought near the free end of the neon lamp, as shown in Figure B, you should see the neon lamp glow briefly. Electrons on the charged balloon move from the balloon to the metal post attached to the free wire lead. The electrons on the metal post cause neon atoms that are nearby to become ionized. When enough neon atoms become ionized, the gas in the neon bulb will conduct electricity. The electrons on the charged balloon move from the balloon through the free wire lead to the metal post attached to it. The electrons are then carried by the ionized gas to the other metal post, which carries them to the wire lead in your hand, which completes the circuit.

The neon bulb does not glow when you connect the leads of the bulb to the terminals of the 6-volt lantern battery, because the 6-volt battery does not have enough voltage to cause the neon gas in the bulb to become ionized. However, the charged balloon has a high enough voltage to cause the neon gas in the bulb to become ionized. On a dry day, a balloon can be charged to thousands of volts by rubbing it in your hair or on a sweater. Even though a balloon can be charged to thousands of volts, the current is low. This is why a charged balloon is not dangerous.

Neon signs used for advertising on stores require 8,000 to 12,000 volts in order to glow. The color of light produced when neon is ionized is orange-red. Other colors can be made with neon signs by using other gases or using colored glass tubes.

Spark plugs are used in most internal combustion engines (except diesel engines) to ignite the fuel and air mixture in the combustion chambers. The principle behind the spark plug is the same as for the neon bulb described above. Electricity at a very high voltage is applied to the spark plug, and the gas between two metal posts is ionized. A spark jumps between the two metal posts, which ignites the fuel and air mixture in the combustion chamber. The distance, or "gap," between the two metal posts of a spark plug is between 0.02 in. (0.5 mm) and 0.04 in. (1 mm). Most spark plugs operate between 10,000 and 20,000 volts.

13

HEAT FROM OXYGEN AND STEEL

HEAT   ENERGY   MATTER

MATERIALS NEEDED

Clear plastic cup

Fine steel wool

Measuring cup

Vinegar

Clock or watch

Thermometer (out-
door type)

In this experiment you will find out if you can use oxygen from the air and steel wool to produce heat.

Fill a clear plastic cup with steel wool. Be sure to use fine-grade and not coarse steel wool. Pour 1 cup (0.24 l) of vinegar (or enough to completely cover the steel wool) into the cup. Wait about 2 minutes, remove the steel wool from the cup, and pour the vinegar down the sink drain. Observe the temperature of the thermometer. Wrap the steel wool around the bottom of a thermometer, as shown in Figure A. Next, insert the steel wool and thermometer into the plastic cup, as shown in Figure B. Set the plastic cup on a flat surface and watch the thermometer for about 10 minutes.

What temperature do you observe on the thermometer? What do you feel if you touch the side of the cup? What do you see happening to the steel wool?

You should see the temperature rise by 30°F (17°C) or more on the thermometer. You will probably feel that the outside of the cup is warm.

Oxygen from the air combines with iron in the steel wool

FIGURE A

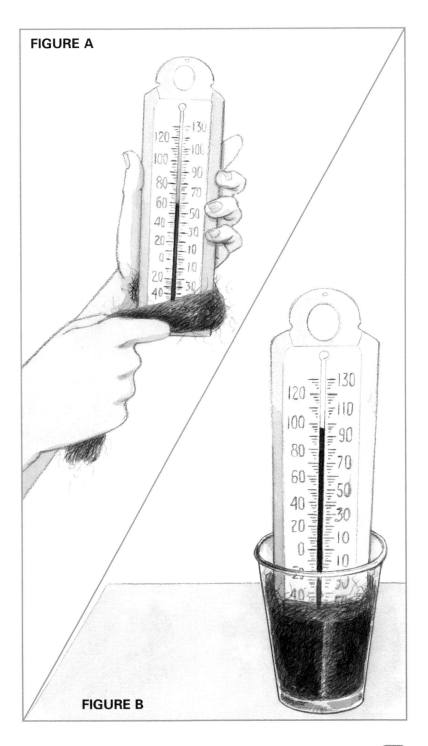

FIGURE B

and moisture to form rust. Rust is a compound of iron oxide and water. You should observe that the surface of the steel wool changes. It probably becomes partially covered by a red or reddish brown coating. This reddish brown substance is rust.

Rust is a solid compound made of iron atoms, oxygen atoms, and water molecules. As your steel wool rusts it produces heat and this causes the temperature to rise on the thermometer.

When metal and oxygen atoms combine, it is called *oxidation*. Oxidation is a process that can cause corrosion, or the wearing away, of a metal. Corrosion costs billions of dollars a year in damage to metal objects such as automobiles, bridges, and ships. It has been estimated that one-fifth of the iron and steel (metal made of iron and carbon) produced each year is used to replace rusted metal.

Corrosion destroys metal surfaces and may form cracks or holes and cause metal parts to wear out and break. Painting iron and steel is one way to help keep these metals from rusting. Paint provides a coating that keeps oxygen and water away from the surface of the metal. Another way to protect iron from rusting and corrosion is by making it into stainless steel. Stainless steel is an alloy, or mixture, made of iron, carbon, chromium, and sometimes nickel. Stainless steel will not rust or corrode. However, since stainless steel is more expensive than regular steel, it is mostly used on smaller objects such as cookware.

Interestingly, the oxygen we breathe from the air is combined with the food we eat to produce energy and run our bodies. This energy is stored and used to run the chemistry going on inside the cells of our bodies. This combination of food and oxygen is a type of oxidation. Like the oxidation of a metal in your experiment, it is a source of heat and energy.

There are small heat packs that are used by campers and hikers to help keep hands and feet warm in cold weather. These packs, using the oxidation of iron powder to generate heat, can produce heat over a period of many hours. Can you think of other changes that use oxygen and produce heat?

14

DISAPPEARING FLAME

HEAT LIGHT MATTER

MATERIALS NEEDED

Candle

Candle holder

Metal baking tray

Matches

Measuring cup

Baking soda

Vinegar

Large glass jar, such
as 32-oz. (approxi-
mately 1-liter) size

❶ **Alert! Adult supervision needed.**

Have you ever seen a fire put out with a fire extinguisher or wondered how a fire extinguisher works? In this experiment you explore why air is required for flames to burn and how a carbon dioxide fire extinguisher can put out a flame from some fires.

Stand a candle in a candle holder. Place the candle holder on a metal baking tray. Light the candle. While the candle continues to burn, add about ¼ cup (60 ml) of baking soda to the bottom of a glass jar. Add ½ cup (120 ml) of vinegar to the jar. Do you observe bubbles forming? Describe what happens inside the glass jar.

Wait about 10 seconds and then tilt the glass jar above the candle flame, as shown in Figure A. Tilt the jar above the flame as if the jar was filled with something you could see and you were pouring it on the flame. However, do not pour out any of the liquid from the jar. What happens to the flame?

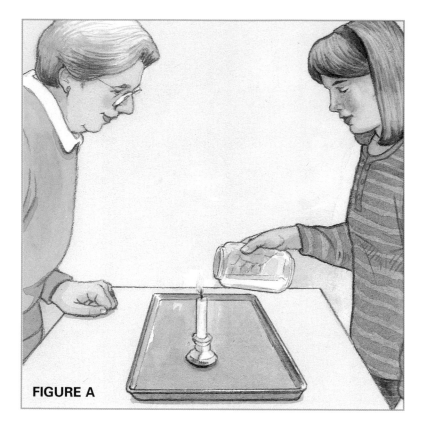

FIGURE A

You should observe that the flame goes out. If this does not happen, try to repeat the experiment. Use slightly more baking soda and vinegar or tilt the jar above the flame more quickly. When you are through with this experiment, be sure the candle is out. Put the matches in a safe place—away from small children.

Baking soda is a solid called sodium bicarbonate. Vinegar is a solution of acetic acid and mostly water. When these substances are mixed together, carbon dioxide gas is formed. Like the nitrogen and oxygen in our air, carbon dioxide is a colorless gas that you cannot see. How could you tell that a gas has formed?

Carbon dioxide gas is more dense than air. An equal volume of carbon dioxide gas weighs more, or has more mass, than the same volume of air. When you tilt the jar, you should see the candle flame go out. The flame goes out because the more dense carbon dioxide gas pours out of the jar and covers the flame. As the carbon dioxide gas blankets the flame, it pushes the air away. Enough oxygen in the air cannot reach the flame and the flame is extinguished, or goes out. If enough oxygen is not present, the flame cannot continue to burn.

The candle flame is a result of hydrocarbons combining with oxygen at a high temperature. The candle wax is made of hydrocarbon molecules, a combination of hydrogen and carbon atoms. The hydrocarbon molecules from the wax and oxygen molecules from the air combine to form molecules of carbon dioxide and water. The starting molecules are broken apart and the atoms rearranged to make new molecules. The new molecules leave the flame as more oxygen enters. This rearrangement of atoms causes the release of energy in the form of light and heat.

The wick in the candle draws up hot molten wax and vaporizes it (converts it from liquid to a gas). Oxygen in the air moves toward the flame. The fuel meets the oxygen, and the rate of burning depends on how fast the oxygen moves through the air to the surface of flame. More than 200 years ago, the French scientist Antoine-Laurent Lavoisier discovered that burning, or combustion, is a rapid combination of a fuel with oxygen. He discovered that oxygen is necessary for burning.

A common type of hand-held fire extinguisher is the carbon dioxide fire extinguisher. It consists of a metal canister filled with carbon dioxide liquid. The high pressure inside the chamber keeps the carbon dioxide as a liquid rather than a gas. When the handle lever is squeezed, it opens a valve that allows carbon dioxide to escape and change to a gas. This gas is directed at a fire by a hose with a funnel on the end, which enables the gas to be spread out over a wider area.

15

LIGHT FROM A BURNING GAS

ELECTRICITY | LIGHT

MATERIALS NEEDED

Candle

Small glass jar or
  candle holder

Metal baking tray

Matches

Piece of screen wire,
  about 5 in. (13 cm)
  on a side

Pliers

❗ **Alert! Adult supervision needed.**

What makes a candle flame and how can it be changed or stopped? In this experiment you will observe the effect of placing a metal screen into a flame.

Stand a candle in a glass jar or candle holder. Place the candle and jar or candle and holder on a metal baking tray. Light the candle. Carefully observe the size, shape, and color of the flame.

Hold the edge of a piece of screen wire (the type used in screen doors) with a pair of pliers. Place the screen wire so it covers the top half of the flame, as shown in Figure A. Keep your fingers away from the flame. Do not leave the screen in the flame for more than a few seconds. What happens to the flame? Move the screen toward the top of the flame. Move the screen toward the bottom of the flame. What do you observe? Blow out the flame. Put the matches in a safe place—away from small children.

Before the screen is placed in the flame you should observe a steady, yellow flame coming to a point about 1 in. (2.5 cm)

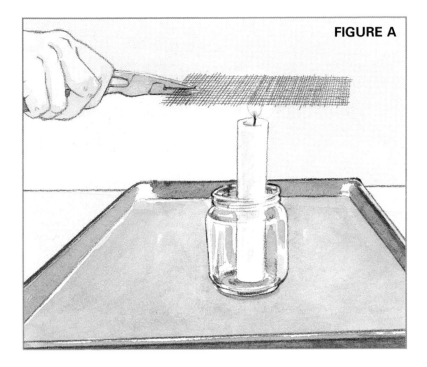

FIGURE A

above the wick of the candle. After the screen is placed in the flame, you should observe that the flame stops at the screen. Does it look like the screen cuts off the top of the flame? Do you see black smoke rising above the flame?

When you move the screen higher in the flame, you should observe that the top of the flame is gone and black smoke rises above the flame. When you place the screen at the bottom of the flame, you should observe white smoke appearing above the screen.

A flame is the light we see when fuel and oxygen combine at a high temperature. This combination of fuel and oxygen is a chemical reaction that converts hydrocarbon and oxygen molecules to carbon dioxide and water. This reaction also produces light and heat. The hydrocarbon fuel and oxygen mix as gases. As long as they mix, the combustion, or burning, continues. In this region of combustion, light is given off.

Hydrocarbon molecules in the candle wax are heated and changed to a liquid. The liquid travels up the wick and is converted to a gas. In the region of the flame, these rising hydrocarbon molecules mix with oxygen from the air and burn. A candle flame is a region of burning gases.

When the screen is placed into the flame, the metal absorbs heat and cools the flame. When the temperature of the flame is lowered, then light is not given off. Even though oxygen and hydrocarbon fuel are mixed together, they do not burn and give off light. The temperature is too low.

The presence of the screen causes the burning, or combustion, to be incomplete. Incomplete combustion causes black smoke to form and rise above the candle. The black smoke is due to tiny particles containing carbon. These particles are called *soot*.

When the screen is placed at the bottom of the flame, white smoke appears. This white smoke is also due to incomplete burning. A smoky flame is due to cracking, a process in which fuel molecules are broken into smaller pieces but there is not enough oxygen to burn these smaller molecules completely.

Soot is a type of air pollution caused by incomplete combustion. Soot is made of small black particles that tend to stick on surfaces. Soot in the air can cause buildings to become dark and dingy. Excess soot can cause the air to become unhealthy to breathe. Have you ever seen black smoke coming out of a truck with a diesel engine? What are some ways that soot can be prevented?

16

JUMPING FLAME

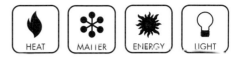

HEAT MATTER ENERGY LIGHT

MATERIALS NEEDED

Two candles

Two small glass jars
or candle holders

Metal baking tray

Matches

Clock or watch

❶ Alert! Adult supervision needed.

Have you ever seen a flame jump from one candle to another? In this experiment you explore what happens when a burning candle is brought close to another candle.

Stand each candle in a small glass jar or in a candle holder. Place the candles and jars or candles and holders on a metal baking tray. Light the two candles and allow them to burn for about 4 minutes.

After 4 minutes, blow out one of the candles. Immediately move the flame of the second candle into the path of the smoke leaving the first candle, as shown in Figure A. The flame of the second candle should be about 0.4 in. (1 cm) away from the wick of the first candle. The smoke may be going directly up or drifting to the side of the candle. Make sure the flame is placed into the path of the smoke. Watch the flame. What happens?

When finished, blow out both candles. Put the matches in a safe place—away from small children.

You should see the flame jump from the second candle and light the wick of the first candle. In this experiment, the flame

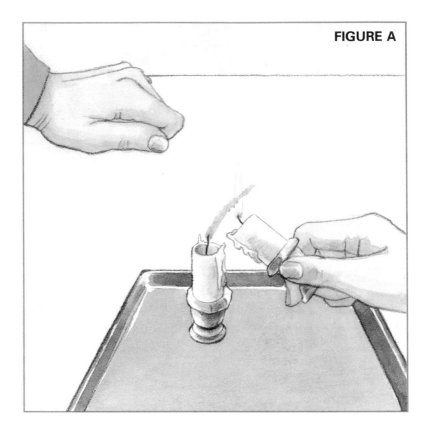

moves through the space between the candles. Because you have just blown out the first candle, it still has fuel around the wick that can burn. The flame from the lit candle can move through this space and ignite the first candle because of this fuel in the air.

In a candle, hydrocarbon molecules making up the wax are heated and changed to a liquid. This liquid wax flows up the wick. The heat of the flame converts this liquid to a gas. The hydrocarbon gas from the candle and oxygen gas from the air combine above the wick. As a result, we see a cone-shaped region of light above the wick.

When you first light a candle, how close do you have to hold a match to get it to burn? When a candle is first lit, some of the candle wax must get hot enough to melt to a liquid before the candle will burn. Because the wax must be hot, you have to hold a match directly on a cold candle. A flame will not jump to a cold candle because there is no fuel already in the air.

In a flame, a fuel and an oxidizer combine in a chemical reaction that produces light and heat. Usually the oxidizer is oxygen in the air. The fuel is something that will burn. The fuel could be a solid such as coal dust, a liquid such as jet fuel, or a gas such as methane (natural gas). The kindling temperature is the minimum temperature required to begin the burning process. In a flame there is a high temperature combination of fuel and oxygen to make new molecules of carbon dioxide and water.

A flame can move through a space filled with fuel and oxygen. Or the fuel and oxygen can move to a flame that stays in one place. The place where the fuel and oxygen combine and burn is called the *combustion zone*.

Flame movement occurs because fragments of molecules that have extra energy trigger combustion in adjacent layers of a fuel and air mixture. A flame can move up to 18 in. (46 cm) in a second. This ability of a flame to move through a space filled with fuel is an important safety consideration.

Liquid can vaporize, or change to gas, even at room temperature. Therefore, an open container of a flammable liquid can release a dangerous amount of gas into the air. The flash point of a liquid is the temperature at which there is enough vapor in the air to make a mixture that could burn. A spark could ignite the space filled with this mixture of fuel vapor and air. This could be a mixture of as little as 1 percent fuel vapor and 99 percent air. Because of this danger, flammable liquids such as gasoline must be stored in safe, airtight containers so no vapor is released into the air.

SCIENCE CONCEPTS

CONCEPT	PAGES
	9, 12, 16, 19, 22, 26, 29, 33, 48, 51, 57
	36, 48, 57
	41, 44, 51, 54, 57
	12, 19, 22, 33, 48, 51, 57
	36, 38
	41, 44, 54

FURTHER READING

To explore further the properties of air and other gases:

Cooper, Christopher. *Matter.* New York: Dorling Kindersley, 1992.

Darling, David J. *From Glasses to Gases: The Science of Matter.* New York: Dillon Press, 1992.

Jennings, Terry. *Air.* Chicago: Childrens Press, 1989.

Mebane, Robert C., and Thomas R. Rybolt. *Adventures with Atoms and Molecules: Chemistry Experiments for Young People.* 4 vols. Hillside, New Jersey: Enslow, 1985–1992.

——. *Environmental Experiments About Air.* Hillside, New Jersey: Enslow, 1993.

Newton, David. *Consumer Chemistry Projects for Young Scientists.* New York: Franklin Watts, 1991.

——. *Science-Technology-Society Projects for Young Scientists.* New York: Franklin Watts, 1991.

Peacock, Graham, and Cally Chambers. *The Super Science Book of Materials.* New York: Thomson Learning, 1993.

VanCleave, Janice. *Janice VanCleave's Chemistry for Every Kid.* New York: Wiley, 1989.

INDEX

ABOUT THE AUTHORS

Rob Mebane teaches chemistry at the University of Tennessee at Chattanooga, where in 1990 he was a recipient of the Student Government Outstanding Teaching Award. He is the author of many articles in scientific journals and, with Tom Rybolt, has written fifteen nonfiction books for young people. Dr. Mebane lives in Chattanooga, where in his leisure time he enjoys white-water canoeing, backpacking, and cooking.

Tom Rybolt holds a doctorate in physical chemistry and is also on the faculty of the University of Tennessee at Chattanooga. He has written extensively for scientific journals, and in 1991 he was a recipient of the Student Government Outstanding Teaching Award. He lives in Chattanooga with his wife, Ann, and their four children, and enjoys reading, running, and raising children.